T0315686

NOTES

ON THE

FRENCH HORSE-BREEDING

AND

REMOUNT ORGANIZATION.

COMPILED DURING A BRIEF VISIT TO FRANCE
BY THE DIRECTOR OF REMOUNTS, APRIL 1914

FIRESTEP
Editions

www.firesteppublishing.com

FIRESTEP
Editions

FireStep Publishing
Gemini House
136-140 Old Shoreham Road
Brighton
BN3 7BD

www.firesteppublishing.com

First published by the General Staff, War Office 1914.
First published in this format by FireStep Editions,
an imprint of FireStep Publishing, in association with
the National Army Museum, 2013.

NATIONAL
ARMY
MUSEUM

www.nam.ac.uk

ISBN 978-1-908487-71-1

Cover design FireStep Publishing
Typeset by FireStep Publishing
Printed and bound in Great Britain

Please note: *In producing in facsimile from original historical documents, any
imperfections may be reproduced and the quality may be lower than modern
typesetting or cartographic standards.*

NOTES ON THE FRENCH HORSE-BREEDING AND REMOUNT ORGANIZATION COMPILED DURING A BRIEF VISIT TO FRANCE BY THE DIRECTOR OF REMOUNTS, APRIL, 1914.

1. CONNECTION BETWEEN HORSE-BREEDING AND REMOUNT DEPARTMENT.

The production of sufficient horses of suitable type to meet the military demands both in peace and war has long been the object of anxious solicitude in France.

The breeding of horses of all kinds is directed by a most efficient branch of the Ministry of Agriculture, staffed by highly-trained professional enthusiasts. Their avowed aim is to guide production along sound lines which shall provide for the requirements of the agricultural population the horses best suited to the soil, and the most profitable to breed, but without losing sight of the essential object of the whole organization, *i.e.*, that horses used in civil life shall be of a type suitable for the supply of the army's requirements for war.

The Minister of Agriculture has the advantage, in shaping his equine policy, of the advice of a Joint Council of Horse-Breeding Department and remount officials, which includes, further, the most prominent civilian breeders of horses of various types.

The working connection between the Horse-Breeding Department and the Army Remount Service is, moreover, very real and close.

The organization of the latter is specially designed to fulfil the State's obligation to purchase as many as possible of the annual contingent of remounts direct from the man who has bred them under the guidance of, and with means supplied by, the Department of Horse-Breeding.

2. OUTLINE OF HORSE-BREEDING DEPARTMENT'S ORGANIZATION.

General Scheme for Provision of Stallions.

First established in 1639, the system of State aid for horse-breeders has continued, with varying success and with only one break (*i.e.*, during the Revolutionary period), till the present day.

The Loi Organique des Haras, passed in 1874, established the system as it now stands.

There are six circles (each presided over by an inspector-general) and there are 25 directors and 45 sub-directors and superintendents, with a corps of attendants of various grades called "Palfreniers".

(B153)   500   5/14   H&S   791wo

Within the circles are 25 stallion depôts containing 3,450 stallions,* of which the most important are at Pin, St. Loe, Tarbes, Compiègne and Pompadour. These depôts serve 756 stations.

The latter has also the only brood-mare stable in France, and there are produced the Anglo-Arab stallions so largely used in the South of France.

The policy of the department is based on a system of zones, the aim being to provide in each stallions of the type best suited to the soil.

For example, at Compiègne, in the Northern Zone, where heavy draught horses abound, the stallion depôt contains only Boulonnais, Ardennais and a few English hackney stallions.

Possibly the breeders would prefer heavy draught horses of Shire or Clydesdale type, but the military consideration forbids ; the Boulonnais and Ardennais are heavy enough for the plough, quick, active, hardy, and live on a comparatively small ration, and, above all, they are suitable for military purposes, for transport and even for artillery, the strain of hackney being intended to increase their activity for this latter purpose.

At Pin and St. Loe, in the Central Zone, where lighter draught horses, high class carriage horses, and the heavy-weight hunter class of saddle horse is produced, the stallion depôts contain thoroughbred stallions, Anglo-Norman or half-breds, Percherons and a few English hackneys.

At Tarbes, in the Southern Zone, we find nothing but Anglo-Arabs and thoroughbred stallions, and the use of heavy sires is absolutely forbidden.

Privately-owned Stallions.

In addition to the 3,500 sires maintained by the State for service at nominal fees, there are three classes of privately-owned stallions standing for public service. In 1911 their number was 8,140.

(a.) *Approved stallions* (total, 1,736)—

  (i.) Those whose covering fee is over 4l. get no premium.

  (ii.) Those whose covering fee is less than 4l. receive premiums from a minimum of 300 francs (12l.) in the heavy draught class to a maximum of 2,000 francs (80l.) in the thoroughbred class. The premium depends on the value of the produce got by the stallion. 30,000l. is the sum thus distributed annually.

(b.) *Authorized stallions* are not good enough to win premiums but are good enough to have a formal certificate of excellence.

(c.) *Accepted stallions* are certified as free from hereditary diseases, but that is all.

Without such a certificate no stallion of any breed is permitted to travel or stand for public service.

---

* 545 thoroughbreds (Arab, Anglo-Arab, and English).

2,175 half-breds (Anglo-Normands and a few roadsters).

730 draught horses (Percherons, Ardennais and Boulonnais).

Brood Mares.

The provision of brood mares is not neglected. Shows are held in every circle at which, in addition to prizes locally provided the State gives handsome premiums for mares with foal at foot and for young brood mares which it is desired to devote to the stud. Permanent premiums for a certain number of years are given to the owners of these young mares, conditional on their appearance at subsequent shows a certain number of times with foal at foot by a State stallion.

Personnel of the Stud Department.

The stud department is not easy to enter and the officials are, in this democratic country, invariably gentlemen of good family.

The training is thorough; after 2 years at the College of Agriculture candidates may compete for the three stud department vacancies offered annually. Successful competitors must have proved not only their agricultural knowledge but their aptitude for the special duties of the department. They then go through a 2 years' special course at the Haras du Pin, which includes a study of the characteristics of all equine breeds, of the objects of and results obtainable by judicious mating, practical care of stallions, foaling mares and young stock, veterinary studies, shoeing, dietetics, treatment, &c.

The lectures are carefully chosen and the students have the advantage of observing the management of a mixed stud of 300 stallions in the most important breeding circle of France.

Finally, students complete 3 years' service with mounted branches of the Army, where they learn the work demanded of the animals in the production of which they are to spend their lives.

The director of a district has arduous and responsible duties. First, he has the care of the stallions in his depôt, where he himself resides, usually in some charming old royal château, the property of the State.

During the autumn and winter he and his staff tour the district inspecting, holding meetings of breeders, advising them as to the care of their young stock and the mating of their mares, and gathering information to guide them in the distribution of the stallions for the following year

In the spring he sends out his stallions in groups to out-stations in charge of the corps of "Palfreniers." These are all old soldiers, ranging from the ordinary stable helper to the stud groom, who takes charge of a group of stallions at an out-station.

The communes apply for a certain number of stallions to serve their district, and are responsible for supplying suitable accommodation both for the horses and their attendants.

The stud grooms in charge of detachments have considerable responsibility financially and otherwise, and the director and his staff are constantly on tours of inspection.

A 2

Finally, the stud officials attend all horse shows and preside over the distribution of the State premiums for mares, &c.

Arab Stud at Pompadour.

The only real national stud in France is at Pompadour, where are maintained 50 brood mares of pure English thoroughbred, pure Arab, and Anglo-Arab strains.

There are also 100 stallions, which serve the surrounding district as well as the Pompadour mares.

The French have a tremendous opinion of the Anglo-Arab as a war horse, and it is to keep up the supply of sires of this type to serve the Southern Zone of France that the stud exists.

The two Eastern Arab stallions I saw did not strike me as of the type which we are taught to look on as the highest "caste," but their effect on the progeny is very marked.

Every precaution is taken to develop the young stock and give them bone, by liberal dressing of their pasture and careful feeding as soon as they can eat.

As 3-year olds they are put in training and tested for speed and stamina.

The surplus mares are sold by auction and command high prices for the known worth of their particular strains of blood.

The colts which are deemed unworthy to become sires are castrated and go to the Remount Department.

The establishment is maintained on lavish lines, and is one worthy of the French nation.

General Remarks.

Breeding in France is at present in a transition state.

In Normandy, the most important breeding district, very high class carriage horses used to be produced in large numbers.

Motors have destroyed this industry, and this foundation stock of big upstanding carriage mares is being used more and more to mate with thoroughbreds to secure true cavalry horses. The present cuirassier horse, which seems to me altogether too big for war, will doubtless lose in size and gain in quality, and a first-class cavalry horse will result. In France the army is always up against the fact that it is practically the only large buyer of saddle horses, whereas we fortunately have the hunter market to keep our breeders busy.

However, all French remount officers say that the quality of their cavalry remounts is improving, though they cannot breed the bone and substance that Ireland produces.

At their great horse show in Paris, the height, girth, weight and bone of the saddle horse is given in the catalogue. A 16-hand saddle horse rarely has as much as 8 inches of bone, weighs more than 1,050 lbs., or girths more than 74 inches. Undoubtedly the best French cavalry horse is the Anglo-Arab, which though light to look at is extraordinarily enduring.

Provision of Funds for the Upkeep of the Stud Department.

When one studies the elaborate organization devoted to the guidance and stimulation of the horse breeding industry, one naturally wonders where the money comes from.

The reply is from racing, the collection being made through the pari-mutuel or totallisator which so largely supplants the bookmaker on French racecourses, and which pays a percentage to the State.

Racing in France is thus compelled to fulfil its duty to the State, *i.e.*, the improvement of the national breeds of horses.

Two year old racing is discouraged, and long distance races and steeplechases are looked on with favour.

In short those responsible for the government of the French turf seem to pay more regard to the national aspect of racing than do similar authorities in England.

3. ORGANIZATION OF THE REMOUNT DEPARTMENT.

The Remount Department includes—

(1.) A directorate at the War Office.
(2.) Inspectors in charge of remount circles.
(3.) Superintendents of the purchasing remount depôts.
(4.) Officers attached to these depôts as purchasers.
(5.) Superintendents of " Annexes " or establishments for the storage of young remounts till ready for issue. (These are normally veterinary officers.)
(6.) Personnel of remount depôts. Total five companies, of which 4 are distributed among depôts and one serves the military college.
(7.) Personnel detached from mounted corps for service at the " annexes."

The purchasing depôts are located to serve the districts where horses are bred, *being designed primarily for the encouragement of horse breeding by the purchase of young horses direct from breeders.* Based upon reports received from remount circles, an allotment is made every year by the remount directorate showing the number of horses to be purchased by each depôt, the corps to which they are to be posted, and the annexes at which those under 5 years old will be stored and matured.

This allotment is subject to modification as the purchase proceeds.

Purchasing is carried out by committees of three officers, of which the superintendent is president—

(*a*.) At the depôt on a certain number of days in each month throughout the year.
(*b*.) During regular tours of the surrounding district from 1st July to 1st March.
(*c*.) At fairs and horse shows, and wherever horses are gathered together.

The depôt superintendents are responsible for arranging and advertising these tours, which are designed to tap all centres of breeding, and bring the market as much as possible to the farmer's door.

The civil authorities co-operate, and the advertisements indicate exactly the type of animals required and the conditions of purchase ; no purchase is final till after the veterinary inspection which follows the arrival of the animal at the remount depôt or other military establishment to which he is consigned.

Horses are bought from breeders at the following ages—

> All chargers, and cavalry and horse artillery troopers usually in October, when rising 4 years old ; but sometimes the purchase is authorized to begin in July.
>
> Field artillery troopers from 1st January on which they become 4-year olds.
>
> After 15th November the army buys thoroughbreds aged 2½ which have been in training—these are horses considered unlikely to win races which owners prefer to sell to the army cheap than risk their purchase in the open market by a rival trainer.

The thoroughbred mares usually go direct to regiments as chargers ; the colts are first castrated at a remount depôt.

No horses are bought from dealers under 5 years old, and French remount commissions never go abroad to purchase.

Especially this year, owing to increase of establishment, a number of foreign horses have been bought from dealers in France, among them some 2,500 Irish and English horses.

The freight and import tax come to 9*l.*, so there is not much profit in the business for English dealers at French trooper prices.

The few horses I saw in the depôt at Montrouge were officers' chargers, and appeared to me to have been cheaply bought at 55*l.* to 64*l.*, considering their age and the freight and import tax.

They included a nice quality 6-year old Irish hunter up to 14 stone, with a docked tail, 62*l.* ; a stout 5-year old 15·1, of no great quality, bought for artillery, but up to weight and a good mover, going out as a charger, 55*l.* ; a 6-year old horse Colonel Ferrar would have bought for R.H.A., 60*l.* ; a weight-carrying grey hunter with good mannners, probably a sale yard bargain, 7 years old, 64*l.*

The heights are :

Cuirassiers	...	15 hands 1 inch to 16 hands 1 inch.
Dragoons	...	15 hands to 15 hands 2 inches.
Light cavalry	...	14 hands 2½ inches to 15 hands 1 inch.
Artillery	...	15 hands 1 inch to 16 hands.
Infantry chargers	...	14 hands 2 inches to 15 hands 1 inch.

The prices this year are for chargers :

					£
Cuirassiers	...	...	...	...	71
Dragoons ...	...	...	...	...	60
Light cavalry	...	...	...	...	54
Staff chargers	...	...	...	...	60
Infantry { Horses	...	...	...	...	44
{ Cobs ...	...	...	...	...	30
Special horses for Military Colleges—					
School horses...	...	...	...	...	56
"Chasers" ...	...	...	...	...	72

Prices for troop horses are :

			£
Cuirassiers...	...	...	51
Dragoons ...	...	...	44
Light cavalry	...	...	38
Draught horses	...	...	40

The total number to be bought in 1914 is 15,500 horses.

I was informed that about half the annual remount contingent is bought from breeders, the rest from dealers.

The breeding of horses bred in France is always entered on the rolls at purchase, and is carefully preserved and always known in the regiment.

French law permits the return of all horses within 9 days from date of purchase which may be found to suffer from certain diseases and vices, *i.e.* :—

> Intermittent lameness.
> Chronic roaring.
> Crib-biting and wind-sucking.
> Jibbing.
> Intermittent ophthalmia (30 days).

After purchase horses are usually sent to a remount depôt, of which there are 17. There they remain under veterinary observation for not more than 20 days before being drafted to their corps, or if under age to the annexes attached to the depôt.

If, however, it is cheaper to send aged purchases direct from the place of purchase to their corps, it is done.

Issues are therefore made as follows :—

Five-year old horses are issued as they are bought, either direct from place of purchase, or after 20 days' sojourn in a depôt. Horses under 5 years old are issued in one batch in October from the annexe where they have been for a year or less since their purchase.

Four-year old thoroughbreds are sent direct to regiments, as also are any half-bred horses which work and hard food may have rendered fit to commence their training.

The utmost latitude is allowed in remount depôts as regards diet and clothing of remounts to ensure their gradual return from sale condition to normal health, and the hygiene of these establishments, through which horses are constantly passing, is always the subject of anxious care.

The stables are invariably roomy, light and airy, and there is plenty of them. The service of the depôt is carried out by cast horses.

4. ANNEXES TO REMOUNT DEPÔTS.

The establishments where young horses are matured for issue are either on Government land, as at Chalons, or on land the property of communes or individuals. In the latter case either the existing farm buildings are adapted, or the owner undertakes their erection according to the approved pattern plan, and the State pays an inclusive rent for the whole on a long lease. The Government appear to have been recently pinched over the renewal of some of these leases, and prefers owning its depôts if possible.

The annexes (except that at Chalons) are attached to and superintended by the remount depôts. They are in immediate charge of a resident officer, either a captain of cavalry or, more frequently, a veterinary officer.

The personnel consists of a warrant officer, non-commissioned officers and men drawn from the mounted corps to which the young horses will eventually belong.

The men are all grooms, jockeys, or farm labourers, and come direct to the annexes, where they complete their service without even joining their regiments. Annexes are all managed on the same lines, though in some the accommodation is more convenient than in others.

The horses are not usually grazed ; it is only the thin and delicate animals for whom any grass is reserved.

Animals are divided into stables of 40, which always remain together and separate from the other batches.

The 40-horse stable consists merely of four light walls, a cement flooring and a tiled roof ; there are two large doors in the middle and mangers and hayracks and rings all round.

The 40 horses are always brought in for the night, the whole stable being bedded down and the horses turned loose.

They are always fed in the stable, tied to the rings ; there are no bales or other divisions, but the hind shoes are off and they stand quietly together.

There is only one man to 10 horses, so the work is confined to keeping the stables clean, feeding and watering, and the animals spend most of their time in the paddock, coming in to feed and to escape the sun, flies, rain or cold.

In every annexe is an exercising track round which each lot of horses is driven daily for exercise.

Before departure for their regiments the horses are tied up for a great part of the day and handled and brushed over.

They certainly look well and are quiet. Sick horse accommodation is supplied in the proportion of 10 per cent.

5. Special Arrangements made by the Remount Department to encourage and assist Horse Breeding.

(1.) *Purchase of Young Mares.*

The remount service is authorized to buy in March and April 3-year old mares, which would not ordinarily be bought till October, but which are specially suitable as brood mares. These mares are paid for, but are left with their breeder, or, failing him, with some other reliable breeder to be put to an approved State stallion and to produce and wean a foal in two successive years ; the mares finally join their regiments in the autumn when rising 6 years old.

Careful arrangements are made for the inspection of the mares, and premiums are given for good care bestowed on them amounting to not more than 10*l.* for the first year and 18*l.* for the second year. These maxima are reduced to 6*l.* in each case if the mare is barren. The produce is the unconditional property of the breeder.

Mares which prove to be in foal after purchase are given to breeders till the foal is weaned for their keep (the produce becoming the allottee's unconditional property).

(2.) *Sale of Cast Mares to Breeders.*

Saddle mares which have been cast but are considered likely to make good brood mares are sent back to the depôt that bought them and there sold at a closed auction of approved breeders recommended by the civil officials of the district.

I saw a number of such mares being sold at Montrouge.

Out of 35 mares only about half a dozen were such as our Board of Agriculture would have accepted.

One was an English thoroughbred mare, Miss Pratt, 10 years old and moving quite fairly well, though cast for sprained tendons ; she fetched 20*l.*

Another was a Belgian thoroughbred which fetched 16*l.*, and the other good ones were half-bred Normandy mares cast from Cuirassier regiments—one, 13 years old, fetched 20*l.* The remaining 30 were a very nondescript collection, among them two very weedy little Irish mares. The prices went as low as 5*l.* for a little bit of a Breton roadster.

It cannot be good policy to encourage the production of what must almost inevitably be misfits.

(3.) *Premiums given at Local Horse Shows.*

6,000*l.* is usually taken in Estimates for this service.

The premiums are given to geldings and mares 3½ to 6 years old shown under saddle and purchased by the Remount Department. The amount of the premium varies with the excellence of the animal, and is extra to and quite apart from the purchase price.

In all these cases one-fifth of the premium belongs to the

breeder, who thus frequently benefits quite unexpectedly from what is known as the " pluie d'or."

Points are given as follows :—

    (1.) Conformation, 5 points.

    (2.) Substance and " presence," 5 points.

    (3.) Strength, cleanness, and shape of the limbs, 5 points.

    (4.) Paces, 5 points.

    (5.) " Quality," 10 points.

    (6.) Training, 10 points for horses 5 years and over.

                 5 points for horses under 5 years.

    (7.) Age, 4-year olds 5 points.

         „   5-year olds 10 points.

         „   6-year olds 15 points.

Dealers are excluded from these competitions.

A winner may, if he wishes, relinquish the prize and take an honorary certificate in its place if on reflection he prefers to keep his animal.

(4.) *Good Prices given for 3-year old Remounts bought direct from Breeders.*

The whole remount system is based upon the direct purchase of horses bred in France ; in fact remount depôts proper are called " Dépôts de Remonte Acheteurs."

Prices have been raised by 10*l.* in the last 2 years.

The last rise of 5*l.* took place after the practical completion of the purchases from breeders for the year, yet I am informed that for each horse bought the additional 5*l.* was paid though long after the purchase had been completed. Such care does the French Government take to encourage horse breeding.

6. FRENCH CHARGER REGULATIONS.

General Conditions.

The State undertakes to supply to all officers free of cost the chargers of which they are required to be in possession both in peace and war, except in the case of officers of general's rank who are charged 15 francs a month for each Government charger in their possession.

Officers are permitted to provide their own chargers under certain conditions, instead of selecting Government horses, but they must have them taken on the strength ; general officers can escape the payment of 15 francs per month if they purchase their Government chargers from the State, or buy their own horses in the open market.

The payment in this case, which is the value of the animal, must be made either in one or two equal sums, and though the horse becomes the absolute property of the general the State retains the right of preemption if and when he desires to part with it.

If an officer's horses are *hors de combat* at the time of

manœuvres he can ride a troop horse, but before he obtains this permission he must be in possession of his full complement of horses. Officers may with the permission of their commanding officer keep one private horse in barracks on rations for which they must pay.

All transactions in chargers are carried out under the superintendence of a regimental committee.

Detailed Regulations.

Charger Committees.—Permanent committees are formed in every mounted corps, consisting of a senior officer as president, a captain, and a veterinary officer.

The duties of the committee are to hand over chargers to officers ; to receive back into the ranks horses no longer required ; to sell chargers to generals who desire to become possessed of them, instead of paying 15 francs per month ; to buy back such Government chargers when generals desire to part with them ; to examine and if approved purchase private horses which officers may produce to be passed in as chargers, and in this case the committees buy the horses and hand them over to officers as their Government chargers.

The committees' decisions are final and there is no appeal.

In buying horses they cannot be too careful to make sure that the horse is suitable and properly trained and quiet with troops of all arms.

The committees must have no hesitation in buying back for the State horses the property of general officers on which the State has a lien, in spite of the fact that the horse is worth far more in the open market, and on the other hand they must not hesitate to refuse any horse which has lost value in the general's hands.

Officers cannot act on a committee when the question of their own chargers is under consideration.

Permission to draw chargers is obtained from generals commanding army-corps, who will be governed by the regulations.

Permission to return chargers is given by the same authority. These permissions are available for 3 months only.

Sources from which Chargers are drawn.

General officers who do not obtain their chargers by private purchase or from the ranks are permitted to take them from the Cavalry School at Saumur, or the Staff College, or from a special remount depôt at Montrouge in Paris, from among a special lot of horses classed as general officers' chargers. Generals of divisions and brigades who have under their command regiments of Cuirassiers are allowed to mount themselves from those regiments.

Officers of mounted corps can choose their chargers from their own regiment.

Mounted officers of dismounted corps are mounted in four classes.

1st Class.—Special chargers. Officers of the general staff, unattached.

2nd Class.—Dragoon and artillery horses. Officers of the general staff attached to corps ; probationers for the general staff ; staff officers not belonging to the general staff ; special general staff attached to artillery and engineers ; officers of dismounted artillery and engineers ; officers of military police ; veterinary officers ; field officers of infantry.

3rd Class.—Light cavalry horses. Intendants ; senior field officers of infantry.

4th Class.—Castrated arabs (equivalent to cobs). Infantry captains and medical officers of junior rank.

For the 4th class there are not sufficient castrated arabs, and failing them company commanders are mounted as follows :— Each light cavalry regiment brings forward every year 7 horses, well trained, quiet, and in every respect suitable as infantry chargers. These are submitted to the judgment of an infantry brigadier, and are then set aside for selection as infantry chargers when required ; if these are insufficient, horses reclassified as unfit for cavalry may be used for this purpose.

Horses thus put aside as possible infantry chargers are considered as extra to establishment of the regiments to which they are attached, and are especially ridden alone and on parades of all arms.

Infantry officers weighing 13 stone and upwards may be mounted on horses similarly selected from dragoon and artillery regiments.

Choice of Horses in Mounted Corps.

When several officers in a mounted regiment require chargers at the same time, they will select them in accordance with the date of their authority ; where several authorities bear the same date, the officers will make their choice in order of seniority.

Officers who are already in possession of one horse will not choose a second until officers who have no horse have made their selection. Medical and veterinary officers will make their selection after combatant officers have been supplied, and they will usually be mounted on grey horses ; in any case the selection must be approved by the commanding officer of the corps to which the horses belong, provided always that no officer shall have to wait more than 3 months dismounted, and that the horses selected are suitable for the officers who take them.

Choice of Horses by Officers of Dismounted Corps.

When the number of horses required exceeds the number of those set apart for the purpose, demands will be complied with in accordance with seniority. In either case the order of priority of choice will be the same as in mounted corps.

Exchange of Horses.

Exchanges between officers may be sanctioned by generals commanding brigades or army-corps on legitimate grounds. The officer on taking over the horse becomes responsible for any depreciation which has not been previously regularly recorded.

General officers when mounted on Government horses which they may have purchased from the State may make exchanges only with the permission of the Minister of War.

Officers changing their corps or appointment may either keep their horses or return them as they wish, with the exception of—

(*a.*) Officers proceeding on foreign service ;
(*b.*) Officers changing from heavy to light cavalry.

Officers proceeding on foreign service who are mounted on private horses can take them with them at their own expense. Officers on leave not exceeding 3 months may take their horses with them at their own expense and are given credit for their forage.

Manœuvres.

No horses belonging to the State may be taken to the manœuvres, if less than 7 years old. Officers whose horses are not available for this cause or by reason of sickness or accident may on production of a veterinary certificate be provided with troop horses.

Purchase of Private Chargers.

Any officer can waive his right to the selection of a Government charger and bring forward in its place a private horse for the Government to purchase and allot to him as a charger under the following conditions :—

Horses must be between the ages of 6 and 8, except thoroughbreds which may be bought at 4, and Anglo-Arabs which may be bought at 5. For eight days the horses will be under observation for soundness, temperament, training, and staying powers ; if at the end of this period the Commanding Officer considers the horse suitable, it will be brought before the permanent charger committee and finally purchased.

General Officers' Chargers.

Government chargers purchased by general officers are handed over at the fixed charger price of their class up to the conclusion of their ninth year ; from the beginning of the tenth year the price is reduced by one-eighth annually, but in no case will the deduction exceed five-eighths.

In every case credit is given for any payment, that is 15 francs per month, already made on account of the horse.

In any case generals become the owners of horses when the monthly payments of 15 francs reach the sum equivalent to the price of the horse. When general officers proceed on foreign service or return home from such service they receive credit towards the purchase of other horses in the new country in which they are to serve, for payments made on account of their horses in the old country.

Care of and responsibility for Government Chargers.

Commanding officers will exercise careful supervision over free Government chargers in possession of officers ; their use in harness is forbidden, and they are on no account whatsoever to be lent to civilians.

Government chargers are handed over to *officers personally*, and officers become responsible for them from the day they are handed over until they are properly relieved of them. When the chargers cease to be required, officers must relieve themselves of the responsiblity by arranging for their return to the ranks unless their successors desire to take them over in the condition in which they may be ; in this case the successor becomes responsible.

Officers are pecuniarily responsible for the loss of a horse if they are adjudged liable ; also for depreciation which did not exist before they took the horse over, and for which they are unable to produce documents relieving them of responsibility. On this account officers in possession of chargers must immediately obtain a certificate signed by the veterinary surgeon, endorsed by the intendant, and accompanied by a report initialed by the commanding officer showing the cause of death, or of accident occurring on duty, or as the result of duty, which caused depreciation to the animal. In case of accidents these certificates are preserved by officers for production on the return or casting of the horses. In case of death or casting, but only when the officer is considered responsible, a certificate must be sent to the Minister of War.

In case of death the certificate must be supported by a post-mortem examination. The casting value if he is cast, or the value of the carcase in case of death, is deducted from the sum which the officer has to pay for the horse.

General officers receive credit for the interest which they have acquired in their chargers in case of their death, casting, or return to the ranks as the result of accidents occurring on duty, but not in the case of accidents occurring in the stable or as the result of sickness. The compensation to be paid will not exceed the price paid for the horse, less a deduction of one-eighth for every year beyond nine.

Return and re-classsfication of Chargers.

Applications to return chargers will only be entertained for military reasons ; horses are not to be returned which ought to be cast from the service.

Re-classification of chargers will be made at the annual inpections by General Officers Commanding, who will detail the corps to which re-classified chargers are to be returned. The charger committees will enter the necessary remarks upon the certificate which permits the return of chargers. Committees, when making their inspections of returned chargers, will be furnished with all the documents and verbal information possible to enable them to make their report. Officers need not be present themselves at this inspection, but must nominate a representative, who will produce all the necessary documents, veterinary history sheets, and so forth, which will relieve them from responsibility for all injuries or deterioration. The Committees will determine what, if any, sum is due from the officers returning horses for depreciation, having due regard to the horse's age and the length and nature of the service which he has performed. Generals commanding army-corps will finally decide upon the sums charged to officers, and will arrange for the payment of the same. Mounted units cannot refuse to receive horses the return of which has thus been duly authorized.

Casting of Chargers.

Horses considered unfit for further service should be cast on the spot by proper casting authorities, and will be sold within 15 days.

Return of the Government Horses obtained from the Remount Department by General Officers on payment.

Horses which generals desire to dispose of must be brought before a charger committee, which will give a certificate that the horse is fit or unfit for further military service, as the case may be. Horses still fit for military service will be bought under the conditions set forth above—that is, at the original price, if not more than 9 years old, and with a reduction of one-eighth for every year's service afterwards. This price must not in any case be considered as the basis of calculation if the horse is subsequently issued to another general officer. If the horse is not considered fit for further service, the general may dispose of him as he likes. Any horse which has been put before and refused by one charger committee, can in no circumstances be shown to another committee.

Heirs to deceased General Officers.

Heirs must give up to the State horses obtained from the Army of which the deceased general may be in possession, and can only dispose of them privately if pronounced by a charger committee unfit for further military service.

7. Census and Classification of the Horses for Impressment.

It is interesting to compare with our own the system of horse classification and impressment carried out in France, where possibly mobilization is regarded by the people more seriously than with us

Early in December each year notices are issued to all horse owners and by 1st January they are legally obliged to attend at the local Mairie and make a declaration giving details of their horses.

This declaration is verified by the gendarmerie and proceedings are taken against anyone who omits or falsifies any particular.

On 20th January an abstract (in duplicate) is sent by each commune to the sub-prefect, who forwards one copy to the district recruiting office. This information must reach the army corps commander by 15th February, and military commissions detailed by him classify the horses between 15th April and 15th June. Certain districts are classified every year and others in alternate years only.

Commissions include an officer of a mounted corps, a veterinary officer and a county gentleman appointed by the prefect.

The commission attends at the Mairie, where all the horses are produced at fixed hours as arranged by the civil authorities, and after examination are classified as cuirassier, dragoon, light cavalry, artillery and so forth, and the classification is entered on the census lists, abstracts of which are eventually sent to the mobilization section of the General Staff. The cost of the census is about 25,000*l.* yearly.

On mobilization a military commission selects the horses required to fill the quota allotted to each commune and payment is made in accordance with the classification of the animal and the price for each class fixed in the budget of the year.